SNARING HEAVEN

To my mother and father

SNARING HEAVEN

Christopher Meredith

SEREN BOOKS

Seren Books is the book imprint of
POETRY WALES PRESS Ltd
Andmar House, Tondu Road
Bridgend, Mid Glamorgan

British Library Cataloguing in Publication Data
Meredith, Christopher
  Snaring heaven.
  I. Title
  823'.914 [F]

ISBN 1-85411-026-8

Cover illustration: The Vela Supanova Remnant, © Royal Observatory,
Edinburgh and Anglo-Australian Telescope Board

*The publisher acknowledges the financial support of the
Welsh Arts Council*

Printed on re-cycled paper.

Typeset in 11 point Palatino by Megaron, Cardiff
Printed by John Penry Press, Swansea

Contents

Acknowledgements

are due to *Poetry Wales*, *Planet*, *Anglo-Welsh Review*, *Planet*, *New Welsh Review*, *Outposts*, *The Gregory Poems 1983-84*, *Poets Against Apartheid*, *Picture: Welsh Poets*, *Social Care Education*, and BBC2 *Closedown* where some of these poems first appeared.

To Gee & Son for permission to publish a translation of R. Williams Parry's 'Y Gwanwyn'.

Also to the Welsh Arts Council whose award of a bursary helped me to complete work on this book.

DESK

I rescued you, splinted your broken legs.
Forty years or so had scummed you dark
With ink, dead skin, the rain of dust, the grease
Of knees and cuffs and fingertips, with work

Done routinely by the bored but paid.
I unlidded you, cut wedges, made true
The skewed split joints, machined human gluten
Off the boards. My carpentry of nails and glue

Fell short of craft but was informed by love.
I plugged you, cleaned your handles, planed,
Saw purity of copper and the packed white grain.
Some wounds were healed, the depth of others learned

—No restoration ever is complete.
People at work, the children and the staff,
Gave you their own disfigurement —
Not inborn malice but the hurt of graft

That rubbed a hole in their humanity.
And I played samaritan out of guilt
Of sorts. Worked out, I was looking for my
Small re-creation as you were rebuilt.

Relidded, drawers eased, your eight legs firm,
Beeswax bringing alive the fans and bars
Of tan and yellow grain, you are a place
For another sort of work. We're both scarred

But the worm in each of us is dead.
I'm not paid much, but neither am I bored
Nor hurt by work's attrition as we go
To real work. This page, the silence, these words.

BREAKING WOOD

Swotting for exams I'd stop at noon
and recreate myself in the yard
with axe and splitting stick for firewood.
The axe was too big, and blunt
from squaring pitprops a hundred years ago
my father said. Still, with a hollow knock and suck
the blocks obediently cracked apart
and light seemed to flow from the white wood
with the sappy fibres smearing a palm
hungry for the not-thought, the not-word.
I'd run a thumbnail in the soft straight grain
or trace the crazing in the marbled bark,
inspire forest that could not be dark
so filled with resin like sunlight.

In my hand the blackened haft was hard,
turned, curved like a femur,
dead like a fern in coal
and the socketed stock wore plates of rust
coat after coat.

This was the history I took to the living wood.
Helve braced against elbow, I was glad
to swing the blade. My father called this good.
In his book it was right, in working men's eyes,
to learn and labour and try to rise.

Like the wood, I knew better but yielded.

In the exams, on wood become dead page
I wrote out thought and word and word
and the past crept in and strangled the light.

Now, from my new home to my old town
I take for my parents wood in the car-boot
Half in apology for what I am.
It has become my turn to hold the book
And my father has the coaled axe for a staff.
He'll put me on some peak or sometimes scoff,
But always we are far, like nodding friends.
Still, each time I wait till the light is gone
Hoping he'll wake, acknowledge me his own.

VIEW FROM THE HILL

From skin and drum and retina
the images come in along the nerves
through dura mater, pia mater
sheathing spinal cord and brain
to the unmade self.

A hand retreats into the coat.
Eyes, wind stung, blur the slabbed grey air,
blur the fretted lines of streets
patterning the dull green trench.
Torn gusts bring and take

dogs' barks, the traffic burr, one child shouting.
Below is everything you are,
animal, machine and child
re-entering along the nerves
through yielding womb walls.

Along the nerves through hard mother,
gentle mother bubbled over spine
and brain the images come in
of the planet turning from the sun,
the clouds dragged clear.

Animal, machine and child stands
remade in overarching dark.
Over a landscape pleated like a brain
the night sky's stretched, punched through
with stars like nerves.

CEFN GOLAU IN SNOW

Some places give almost nothing.
Stare hard and you can almost see
horizons where off-white meets off-white.
The sky can be a wash of greys
and when the wash thins
the sun can rub a pale disc
on a frozen screen.
Dwarf trees can crab like script
against the snow.
Far off, broken places in the ground
make punctuation where
there are no words.

Yet turn an invisible corner on the hill
and down there, estates and towns
blot through in smirched insistent chains.
Clouds shred like battlesmoke.
Colour abrading the eye with its grit
is the houses clinging to the slush lanes,
heaped cars rusting in a compound.

SIX POEMS FOR TROEDRHIWGWAIR

1 In the green lane

This was the not-town:
two sunned terraces under the hill,
the road's end and a path through the trees,
fountain farm and a green lane to the stream.

My mother had played there, she told me,
under the one gaslamp in the lane.

Now, in visits, the countryside to me
unknowably old was there
in nettlechoked railings,
hayboys on the gambo,
dead things found in ditches.

On that rock I was unshakeable
though I saw the shattered lampcase
and the rusted gaspipe
uncoiling like an adder from the earth.

2 Over New Pits

Passing from houses to hill
Through scruboak, hawthorn,
The uncoiling fern

Where whole worlds of pursuit and
Capture linger still
  We reached scree and cliff,

Played where the earth was man-torn,
Where we could unlearn
Our books and stand

Exultant on the high crag
Above Bedwellty Pits.
The crawling antfolk

Did not know this wimberry world
Where we climbers bragged
    Our coats mud-stiff

Or slid down the grassing tips
Till darkness spoke
And the vision curled.

3 Wasps

Visiting. The quiet. Relatives. Dark
Of a kitchen always dark, all chafed against
My learned politeness, eight years old or so,
Wore it thin. This was my mother's home, but
Not quite mine. And Grammer like a mountain
In a black pinny, her face not a face,
A hardening of darkness, something gathered
Worked from a shadow, might open the mouth,
Become a face to drink tea, or sighing
Turn the head towards the grate,
Remark the white ash flaking on the hearth.

Escape was into a drawing-book, or
Into the yard to breathe cool air. One time,
Wasps in a jar on the window-sill
Legs milling slow and helpless in the jam
Held me in the yard's shade under the hill
Long and someone might have said the sweetness
Tricked them into this. Up the high cracked steps
I climbed like a tired swimmer who laps
The salt in gasping for more air.

                              The sun
Exploded on my head and that was to burst
From the cold pond, find heat and raise my arms
And bask in light, warmth rilling on my back.
And in a noon where broken glass, buckets
Without bottoms, a cracked sink, fencing-
Wire in shreds on posts, uselessly slack,
All litter was made permanent, heatstruck
Like a fluted temple, made timeless by
The day, it was unthinkable that such
Perfected steel could rust and blister to a
Sunset avalanching wreckage down a sky.

Up the hill and away from the terrace
The moment cooled under the lightwashed rocks
And after short maturity, congealed.
Thistles erected bloody maces
Boulders that had comforted concealed
A horror like the whiteness of a root
Drawn too easily from a yielding earth
And every bulge and hollow in the slope
Swaggered threats.

                              I, of course, retreated
To the row of shadowed kitchens. It was
No premonition of the riddled hill's
Slipping frightened me, though the place grew frailer:
The street below, younger than two lifetimes,
Brief as mushrooms on a rotten branch;
And Grammer watching ash flake on the flame,
Snared in dark, arthritis-racked, was made less.
Only panic on the treacherous hill
Forced me back into the yard, sent me home.

4 Uncle Billy in the front room

Lemon- and biscuit-coloured light.
The oilcloth under the highframed bed
dusted clean, lightflooded
and me and my younger brother
shy children with the invalid.

We would like a bed pushed in the sun,
a frame like that to keep the blankets
off our legs.

He laughs and makes us exercise,
pedal air. Keep fit, he says.

But this is something absolute and good
and 'uncle' no relation, just his name.
The shrunken man, unshaven, spectacled, thin,
is misread as permanent.
Uncle Billy ambered in light and memory.

So fine to be tubercular like this:
a room with a bed,
a suntrapped, latticed bookcase.

Fixed in light on
a bookspine of a tale of castaways
a hero clambers an exotic hill.

5 *Taking My Mother to Troed*

We saunter along both the rows
And at each door she names a ghost,
The family history and how
They died, or moved, or why they stayed.
Rob Roberts her father, Auntie Ada,
Pen Rogers, George Wimblett like a
Daicapped christ heaving firewood,
Mason's Farm, The Woods, New Pits.
Naming of the haunts and haunters
Somehow fixes things, though names
Like colours come loose in the dark.

On top row a bus turns, empty.
From grass erupting through the tar,
The burnt-out school, the breezeblocked doors,
She looks up to the breaking hill.
'Oh good god, o' course it've moved.'
She wonders at the few who've stayed,
Says she would not go back to this. So
Sadness would be affectation

Making us the passing tourists
Eager to be sentimental
About sheepshit, empty buildings.

6 Larks

Snow retracts in hollows
Above the adit mouth which
Blows rank air under larks climbing.

Houses without people
Lose all sense of self-respect:
Mosses etch the mortar, slates fall

And plaster falls from laths.
The piebald hill shrugs off snow,
Shrugs off people and the walls

Give up and tumble. Cars
Come and callers sup the past
And leave. To give up and be sad,

Like stones, is so easy
Though this is scarcely even sad —
Just random, as where weeds will grow.

Like winddriven midges
We came, clung a moment, went
When economics belched up the drift

With the reek of fear.
Matter is so unheeding
Blame needn't taint the taste of loss.

Yet over Troedrhiwgwair
Larks nail the light with hammered air
Climbing, will-sustained, beyond sight.

IN EBENEZER CHURCHYARD, SIRHOWY

On this grey smear of a weak day
the rasp of a forced gate
explodes impossibly.
Rubbish cast by the wall
blares in the eyes.
In winter light, you think,
it should all break and fade.
Drizzle smudges all the edges
makes eyes thirst for colour
soaks without sensation
makes feet soundless
the air sodden bland and comfortless.
In the grey nothing edges of graves
butt pallidly into vision, geometry
scraped on the rain.

There is no tradition to say this.
Here is no stone tower to crutch
a wrong church nor yew to undermine
with his older root the shallow ruler. Only
a shanty-town of leaning slabs
picked over with a fuss of letters
curled to remember the sweep of a nib.
There quench the eye.
Jane Pryce diweddar o Swydd Feirionydd
dead with her baby and others respectable
only their trades in English
all quietly rubbing to nothing on the air.

The children from the flats
have gone home on their bikes

taken the colour with them
except by the wall on the beaten grass
the busted plastic bag leaks cellophane
and printed cardboard darkening with wet
but clear enough for eyes to seize
to drink from greedily
in a bare place in the rain blur.

So these are the ones who walked from the west.
Twelve shillings a week instead of eight.
Cadernid ffydd.
See the upshot:
rain that runs on the smashed stones
a drinker from a broken cup.

THIS

There's not a puddle by a mountain track
but has some inundation myth
no nook without some gelert dead
and a remorseful master
no waterfall but makes a witch's pool
no place of farms but has some pwca'r trwyn
to suck the kine.

Legend bubbles through the paint like rust
on seaside handrails
shadows the sarn under the sea
in the calipers of a little bay
hinting some other sunken world
or laps like water
at the sleeping watchman's feet
drunk after feasting.

Rocks of armorica
under the grinding sea.
No. No great gulfs, no unknown lands.
This is only a lover on his own
a dowdy, shrunk atlantis,
the curving arms of a little bay embracing
a dream of only another self.

SHEEP

This one, you guess, looking at me, is the leader.
His stare is not a challenge. Nothing. Just a stare.
And the way the others clutter behind him in the wagon.
This, you think, is some photo of an old war. Clothes
ragged, cropped heads, children dazed calling for food,
all the thin legs merded with crammed travel
and eyes indifferent with many deaths.
The eyes, you think, must haunt the guards at compound gate
hinting of seeing through all things.
Perhaps you feel yourself melt a little, feel naked
when I look at you.

We have been a rich vein for you,
for your languages and rites.
Your god was one of us, you say
yet also our crooked captor, caring for us
clinical with our surgery
his outstretched manpicture your mangod picture.
We have been: The Lost, The Wanderers, The Sufferers.
You have set us on high and taken our flesh.
This is no injustice. Only irony.

Sitting with your car door pushed open in the afternoon
one foot on the earth
tea in the flask, a map in the glovebox
you can look around the country where we are kept
and feel no wryness —
feel warmed even, in the dozing lanes
hate the smoke and motorways you came out of
before you turn back.
But you catch my eye a moment on the passing wagon.

Reflected there you see all the rolling vale
your fallen eden unfolded and become
a heaving green belsen.

ON HAY BRIDGE

8.00 pm in a belated spring
in still air under marbled sky
trees stand foot to foot on their reflections.
The river dimpling only over stones
goes glassy at its edge,
is clear beneath me.

A salmon a yard long, dark slate
blotched with sour milk,
twitches against the flow,
sways, mirroring the ropes of weed,
sidewinds, sideslips, tacks upstream.
Gerallt saw her eight hundred journeys back.

The banks no doubt were greengorged then in spring.
In clearings spent homesteads smouldered.
Wooden towers, slowly, were rebuilt in stone.
Castles studded conquerors' intent,
stitched the sleeve with rock.
Lords dead in Gwent. A headless corpse in Cwm Hir.

Three hundred years of gradual collapse
and Bedo Brwynllys near here
sang sweet and politic of loving girls
and how their eyebrows curved
like rainbows or like squirrels' tails.
Namesake, let me not be you.

Eight hundred years and still we say
you lose less by retreat.
Some martyred hero and a moving song

will do to warm an evening perhaps.
In daylight, let the current inch you back
against yourself.

The light, waning, cools mirrored greens
to lave thought, blooms the river with
a promise of opacity. Swallows,
openthroated, trawl the air for flies
beneath the bridge, drive on like the salmon
and let their element wash through.

She, slatemilk, edging out of sight
slides under the reflected trees.
Come back, I think. Come rain
to puncture all reflection.
Give me that pied yard of muscle
to inch against what pushes me from home.

ANOTHER GO AT HAY BRIDGE

Each week at seven I've come back
to this bridge, each time remarked
how the tilting earth shaves away daylight.

There was blue, and the swept bank piled
with trees. Marking flow, weedropes were
intricate with leaves on the pebbled bed

and sprays of cloud came west another time
ruddled, orange, and the pit above
indigo and around me amethyst.

In the corridor of turned trees
I've stood with my head in the skydome
by constant discs of mars and jupiter

and after, the milky way a semen river
washing cygnus and auriga
arched over me.

Now black trees hunch. Beneath in clamming mist
the river's slicked with clouded mercury,
the weeds gashed dark,

                          as the earth,
tilting, pares its minute from the day
and lamps smirch orange globes on air.

I shrink into my coat, turn back.
There'll be frost soon but, too, the pleiades.
Somewhere above the other river runs.

SNAPSHOT

At evening sun boils across
These mountains, makes a show
Of powdered gold and plated brass

That cools to blood, a soft rust glow
Under a crawling green net
Soothing the bronze to shadow.

Or swags of cloud may lift to let
The bleak space briefly speak
From deep inside a freezing skirt

Of acid colours burnt as stark
As winter trees across rise
Before the fading into dark.

As daylight crumbles I suppose
That to know is to become
In time. Places digest those

Who never did intend a home
Just there. But callers declare
They like the view and click a claim,

Knee on sill, with a camera.
The photo's dropped in my lap.
What I would learn with aching care,

Poor becoming, is a weakling's pap,
The poem grown empty, crass,
An easy acquiring, a snap.

ON HIS PHOTOGRAPH OUTDOORS

Who does he think he kids?
He doesn't belong in this and will, soon,
be back in his house on the main road
— so many nozzles on a sewer — consuming
processed cheese and televised snooker.

The place has become less itself
than a space to visit in.
A child's voice fills a moment in the field,
is bloomed with far off silences
or the indifference of traffic sounds.

It has become less itself than a place
where words slip round the nearest tree.
Sometimes he finds their prints
and makes a few blurred plaster casts,
though no one can make much of what they are.

So the poem's a kind of inner sasquatch,
half mocked, only finding credence among
isolated children, like himself.

The world's another planet we explore
in zipped suits, enduring its poison air.
Home's a smudgy nebula within,
light years away, exploded ages since.

THE VEGETABLE PATCH

Every year I turn it over, reluctantly.
The levered spade turns up treasure.
Pink spidery flowers on a plate-lip
Not enough to tell the whole pattern.
A ridged shard. The foot of a saucer, perhaps.
Earthenware a finger thick
Suggests a pantry-slab, stored ale.
The levered spade turns up the dead:
A clay-pipe stem like bone, the marrow sucked,
Thin Victorian china for bits of skull.

Our shelves inside are filled with
Complete sets, in use, neatly arranged.
Sometimes I wonder what we'll leave,
Or whether I'll ever, turning
The blade like this, find all the bits
Of just one plate from some old dresser.
But mostly I wonder whether, this year,
It should be lettuces or spuds.

SNARING HEAVEN

Gardens are mantras
contrived to trap
tranquillity.

What isn't liked,
define as weed.
Voluptuous

the loved things grow, bolt
though ordered mud
in qualified

wantonness. Rose
is just vetch gone
decadent, blown,

disneyfied beyond
passion to glamour —
not transgressing,

though, airspace of neat
beds and borders'
contemplative

geometries. So,
all making made,
contrivances

complete, we walk at
dusk the ranks of
unblotched sprigs in

clean dirt, contemplate,
after work, inspect
the mossless lawns,

our spirits breathing
to the unborn weeds:
you dare, you dare.

SHE PLANS A PURCHASE

Across the table came her photographs.
'This is the garden. This, the view.'
    She faltered then, expected us to scoff.
        We looked up from the snaps and she
        Dropped her eyes defensively.

Dream home. The roseframed door. All that stuff.
For such sophisticated folk
    I'd thought coffee, talk and books would be enough.
        'And here, in the garden, a well.'
        'No gnomes?' Still irony's the rule.

And 'Heaney's got a poem about wells — '.
I bit my tongue. It's not done to
    Be so showy. Literate types don't spell
        Out allusions. Even so, I'm
        Forced to think how place gives way to rhyme.

But her pictures try to fill an aching space,
To hold a certain, living self.
    A hole sunk to the lifesource of a place —
        Or some such phrase — helps her get by.
        These rhymeless ones need places more than I.

SONG

Hearing the catch
I know his parts
And, mechanic,
I hear the click
Of cog and ratchet.

Feeling the flow
I drink her flood
Knowing I hear
Her wrought device
Sing undivided.

SEGOVIA ON RECORD

Fingers trap the moments on the frets
and weave them into coats of sound —
the right hand's hard and glassy at the bridge
or at the soundhole fluting,
the left strokes lovely ramirez's neck,
jigsaws fretted screens at the alhambra,
holds the coat up to be seen

and so

no fingers catch the moments on the frets —
the imageless precision of the coat
masks the weaver's hands; no screen, no thought, no
self, no coat — only limitless technique
worked on a sounding abacus, and always
the black disc spiralling towards its end,
the hiss of time like rain on the roof.

PLANET

Ice white and ice blue, no sci fi chart
Of expectations — green for growth, brown shades
For mountaintops — but ice blue and ice white,
A ball of ice incised by skaters' blades.
Cupped to the globe the figures swirl ice-
Spiders, galaxies link their spirals,
Chain oceans, snag on mountains and embrace,
make frost storms in a gazer's crystal.
In gaps seas glitter colder, coastlines show
Ghostly and paler than ice white, ice blue.
The camera clicks us clicks us so we know
How pale we are as we spin from or to
The night. And africa a tongue of flame
Is curled like a foetus around this form.

MOON THROUGH BINOCULARS

No man in the.
Not galileo's continents and hills.
A diseased eye.
A glare bulging out of dark.
The charred *maria*.
The hot white icesplash by the southern limb.
No metaphor remakes it.

The stories of the mad come clear now
when what's un said un known
stares back unfaceably.

JUPITER

Callisto

chafing the magnetosheathe
frost odalisque

Ganymede

iceballed catamite
pitted with jove's emission

Europa

packed squirming
in the egg's membrane

Io

flexion as of skullplates
between jove and the packed womb
boils the brains
opens sulphur pustules

Zeus

substanceless ammoniac
bloomed with unbearable dark
a raw eye rolling fluids

black lesions in the sour yellow
bubbled with marbling of lardstorms

grs

if there was bone you'd see it

ammonia clouds skimmed
the deep wound scoured
to shredding tissue

worlds across

a weeping ulcer on the lecher's shin

JETS

All day the jets have rifled through the air,
Drilled through the lessons that I've tried to give,
Scabbing the blue with vapour for a scar,
Passing the dummy-bombed hamlets with a wave.

I'm comforted myself. I'm not so bad,
I've thought, in spite of the raised voice, the sudden squall.
If discipline and strictness knocks them dead
At least I'm not out there learning to kill.

And each frail cliché rears to the surface,
Writhes in the strong light, dies, and having sunk
Leaves me to know I work for who in office
Shuts books to put more octane in the tank.

What *I* would does not possess our minds.
This boy, the fat one, has been rifled too.
Belongs to the plane and every bomb it sends,
Absorption melted from his ragged row

Of words. Just now he, my bluntest blade
Inevitably felled first in any game,
Looked from the tortured page, the word-wrought board,
To a sky where steel hammered its own scream —
And smiled.

EXAMINATION

The compass arc makes bubbles
round the jointed polygons.
Eyes, focussed at the nib,
clamp her problem to the page.
Hand at her temple up among her hair
supports the vault of head and curving back.

Last night
              I think, unfocussed,
shifting my weight, feeling
each small itch through double supervision.
My wife.
Hand on the womb-bulb feeling its heat,
the curving well-upholstered fall
to the navel circular and soft,
the nipples erecting to the lips,
the subtle making of our single plait.

Here, singly,
each after each at her desk in the sun —
from elbow to hand, from
hand to her temple up among her hair
to nape, to the arc of back, to the leg
a jointed coil around its twin,
twined feet hooked under plastic seat —
each swept by the clockhand clamps the page,
each works,
a hunched erotic question mark.

EMPTY CLASSROOM

From here, the light aslant a pastel wall,
the usual forgotten coat,
and on the noticeboard a poem — WINTER —
laboriously wrought, illumined with
a smiling yellow snowman.

From there, the sundimmed blackboard, and
on those hidden backs of desks,
stupendous pricks and lovehearts intertwined
in thick black felts.
The tail of childhood slips by unobserved.

Through the window, endlessly
the melt and roll of sky
that covers and discovers random hills.

EVENING

A lover walked along a nettled lane
Past worn fenceposts warm with evening sun
And back-gates smoothed with home's familiar palm
And over green plants forcing through the stone.

She was selfconscious. Prim steps said:
Like this I hope my lust is hidden.
But 'trysting' the step said, 'trysting' the look,
So sex-ache spoke in every stiffened move.

The girl was passion going by
Although she kept her eyes downcast like prayer.
By iron-slag I clutched the rusted railing:
Above lopped trees a lone bird trailed the sky.

MIDDLE-AGED SONG

When I loved a girl
   I could walk in flame
Watch flesh curl
   And not be lame.

Now sense contains
   The fool in me
And lovers' lane's
   An amenity.

WALKERS

See two people walking on the hill.
If I could call a hundred pictures, say,
Or a thousand to live crammed inside your head,
You wouldn't know, if I could do that,
The knotting of the thigh against the slope
Or how the stones and grasses clot the path.

If I could call the planets to your room
And make callisto's ice sheet round your mind
And rend you with the gravity of suns,
You wouldn't know, if I could do that,
The coolness of the wind against their hands,
The steepness of the hill that they walk on.

FORKED TREE

Sap's squeezed from heartwood
in our thickened trunks.
We're two on one root, though
we've leant away in growing
this age past.

There's sunlight sometimes.
Live things come to pester us,
call, flit.
We gesture something close to love,
make them high cradles,
think perhaps they answer our *why*.

When crowns begin to break at last
they'll go for good.

Stretching few leaves we'll
keep the quiet, feel bone whiten, knowing
as we always did
that we lead nowhere except back
to our one self.

A WAITING-ROOM

After midnight, fill another glass.
Today will just be more of the same.
More seed in the palm no longer seen,
Great dawns joining all the rest
In the cellar with sunsets, misty mornings.
Blushing gets harder. Embarrassment
Like pain will go at last.
You know I once held Epicurus strong
And once as well I was adored.
When that stops it makes no odds
If Epicurus was right or wrong.
How ever much it's fun, you're bored.
All making taints itself with this:
The fear of only being.
Action and praise like Sunday hymns
Are the vapour-trail of what's important
Or the crumby magazines we read
As we shuffle bums along a bench
Towards the door of the waiting-room.
The song, the carpentry, the seed,
After the end of true delight
Are habits that affirm or ease
The rolling by of day and night.

NEXT

Somebody's livingroom window has been shattered
the sofa blown askew
the unhinged door pushed flat
where they dragged him out
before the camera came.
Heavy shards of plate glass
lean against the radiator
among the wreckage of
ashtrays, photoframes, small ornaments.
A gout of blood viscous as slobbered custard
lies in a flattened place among the bits.

This in a glance up from my book.
I sniff, bite the sandwich.

Probably dark abdominal stuff, though
the lustreless vtr is imprecise.

The newsreader leafs the page.
Her hand is bandaged.
Sympathetic, concerned, I imagine the hot dish,
the neglected oven glove.

WHAT'S CERTAIN

On an altar in some chancel things,
Perhaps, are solved. There are people, no doubt,
Who've seen truth reified, made if not flesh
Then some profound geometry that can
Be grasped, imaged revolving on a screen.
Door after door approach the last chamber
Where the plot of humankind unravels.
And we haul in the cord to a roman gallows
Or, romantic, to some waterfall or hill
Or, more recently, to a placenta
Suckered to the wall. Artful that, making
The ultimate ultimate defilement.

That squally day the publisher — part time —
Talked hard in the carpark. We diagnosed
Where welsh lit in either tongue fell short.
I don't know what we said. Behind his specs
He squinted. I was reticent as we
Did some arcane verbal dance and parted.
I paused at the docks, then, of the mudslicked
Port the coal left from, saw small boats
Keeled to forty-five degrees and rotted
Scaffolds gulled and upright on the lead-grey
Tidal mud. Far off a plate of sea
Like stainless steel sent glimmerings.
Knowing, I thought, my road, I drove homeward
Up the merthyr motorway through mizzling
Rain scythed by the wiper in a greaseslick
On the screen. And on a rise suddenly
A rim of lit upland opened, spread to
The speed of the car. The beacons unfurled

A ribbon tawny in far sun, swelled
In the scoured air, peaked stiff, scooped and curled
As snowdrifts. Silence. Then wipers scythed again,
I heard the engine purring in its case.
The band of mountains faded like a match.

My mother made good meals I couldn't eat.
I sat by her window looking at my car,
The clock, thought of my wife and sons, feeling
Not at home but in a waiting-room.
He was a long time and I went to check,
Hesitated at the plastic curtain.
He sat where he'd slipped in the bath, his arms
Flung out, the white breasts folded on his paunch
Like a chinese buddha or a newborn child.
The lathered hair was peaked stiff and curled, scooped,
Pale gold as chewed-tobacco phlegm. And far
In his throat the breath-words — *I'm all right, I'm* —
Faint through the hiss of the waterjet.
And there I saw the cataract and hill
Again, a gallows and an empty womb
Transformed to buckled man, to condensation
Streaming on the tiles.
                              The doctor clipped
His instruments away selfconsciously,
Went, saying, tactfully, that we should
Call him in an hour or so, either way.

One hour we pumped every time he stopped,
Observed meanwhile the irrelevance of
All the rubbish cluttered in a day, of

Wardrobes sheathed in plastic walnut. Outside
We saw rain falling far on troedrhiwgwair
In crawling bands.
                    Not this time. He came back,
Ate even, talked of news and politics,
What literature can't do to save the world,
And cash. Of where he'd visited, no word.
Guts or its opposite held us all back.
But in our heads were random echoes
Making harmonies of rain and light,
The facts of meat and pain and nothing else.

SPRING

After the Welsh of Robert Williams Parry

After the weather cold and dull
    And the ice like fire burning,
After the roping of the bull
    And the weary hours of churning,
Spring gives lighter work to me
    As the air grows mild again,
The blade slips oh so easily —
    The lambs do not complain.

When I see at my hand the slaughter
    Of a curled fleece in the mud
Why should I weep water
    For the shedding of such blood?
After living thin and needy
    Through many a winter's day
Some Christians will dine sweetly
    At my feast on their Sunday.

NOTES FOR A NOVEL, PERHAPS

Of reaching into dark.
Of sunlight on leaves.
Of the man caught in the rattled burst.
Of few, few.
Of prayer, of sorts.

*

Once he took me in the pulpit with him. I was still too little for
my head to show. He talked and talked. I looked up his back
which, I knew, inside his suit was unwashed from yesterday's
turn. The dark grained into it. The man talking and a window
and a tree, his face all light, about rising. That one day a week
and the rest the dark working on the spine.

*

Few, few shall part where many meet

The words as beautiful as tears
tie memory to memory.
Slats of light across a classroom wall.
The teacher makes them chant
punishes those who can't.

Few, few shall part where many meet
The snow shall be — shall be —

— Yes you duffer. Use your head.

His knuckles whiten through the fat.

*

He hated the journey into dark
that walk
the cage
the fall
stable
stall
the dark impacting on the eye.

Reach into the dark.
There.
Not inner dark — save metaphors for sundays —
but the clamped rock prised.
Reach into the dark to fetch what makes
our civilization tick
the darkest stuff clawed out
and made to burn.

*

Sunlight through leaves.
The green bench slatted,
enscrolled cast iron endframes
· warm in june,
the bandstand's apex of the park's
ornate chinoiserie.
A quiet place for a schoolboy to smooth
the book, to see in unaccustomed sun
the grain of paper,
smell the binding.

The old men on the next bench argued.

— I tell you I remember —

— No. I was twenty-one. The year
the franco-prussian war broke out.

So how old?
He did the sums.
The backward chasm opened under him.

*

Few, few shall part where many meet
The snow shall be their winding-sheet
And every turf —

Words soothing as slowmoving skies
in summers on the edge of fields.

He loved to read. Peter Wimsey, Marx.
Words lovely as the taste of aniseed.
Ideas made flesh he played the male game
pretending to know how the world works,
striking poses by a mantelpiece.
Fighting fascism the only way
and a way from dark,
the stench of shale and sweat.

*

I found a chapel. *Methodistiaid* on the wall outside. I could
understand that much. People all familiar sat inside speaking
words I couldn't understand. I felt selfconscious in the uniform

but it was better than the shit in a surplice at the camp. Warm handshakes and the quiet word. The laypreacher holding my hand a little longer, farewelling, switches quick but awkwardly to english. — The south? he says. And there are weary lines around his eyes as he smiles in the sunlit doorway and his gaze drops to my epaulettes.

*

We will kill
without fear
without remorse
without dread

we will —

— Go on, repeat, the small arms instructor said,
american, something big in prohibition days

— kill
without fear
without remorse
without dread

and they may have half laughed then
but said

without fear
without remorse
without dread

because they thought, imagined, saw,

presumably, some need of prayer
and so they said

we will

      kill

without   fear
without   remorse
without   dread.

— So. Say that every night, he said

we will

    kill

    fear

    remorse

    dread.

Urbane and with academic stoop
he stopwatched them at kicking doors
filleting dummies with
the automatic rattled burst.

*

Hairnostrilled as a dickens stepfather he
sprays halitosis on the boys

knuckles whitening through fat
and recitation turns into escape
a sort of prayer or sugar stick.

Few, few shall part where many meet
The snow shall be their winding-sheet
And every turf beneath their feet
Shall be

Words soothing as slowmoving skies
In summers on the edge of fields.
A rhyming art to salve the eyes
With visions of heroic worlds,

With words that scroll as artfully
As balustrades along a bay
Where sunlit seas glint prettily
For happy boys on holiday.

*

At night it's cold. The battledress is thin.
We didn't bargain for the hill, the night.
There were the swamps
and wading in thin mud
filling the canteens with the crawling scum,
blown corpses rolling in the current
all that.
On the hill we're hungry
but have supped full of.

And then clangour. Voices.

— Souse that light.

I didn't know where the light came from
and shouted again

— Souse that light.

But he rose a spreadeagled sun
staggering, his arms flung out
and I didn't know where the light came from
till I saw the man burn in a phosphorus bomb
caught in the rattled burst. He
collapsed beyond a parapet
left a twilight and then dark.

A close mortar and the mountain jumped
like a hammered tabletop.

Me and my mate crouched in the scoop of earth
said nothing till a lull
and then I called to him.

Reach into the dark.
His head had been there seconds since
the carotids piping life
eyelids blading moisture on the lens.
And lower.
There. Reach.

*

You've seen the newsreels. I've never seen a crowd like that, and in it all I was the enemy. Only shorts and shirt, but still they're khaki — cachu my mother says — and the beret, and the boots absurd and heavy. So many thousand quiet, not even the children calling after me, curious for a touch of ginger hair. The thin man in a sheet and spectacles raises an arm, begins in hindi. I've read the books. I used to like reading. I have an idea of his theme but I stand with a rifle, not understanding the words.

INTRICATE MAY

After a medieval Welsh fragment

Intricate May the loveliest month.
    Birds' clangour. Branches writhe and wind.
The ox in yoke. Ploughs rutting earth.
    Green ocean and the mottled land.

When cuckoos call on greening trees
    Grief hurts the worst.
Smoke in the eye, long sleeplessness
    For kinsmen lost.

PRISONERS

Nyt oes le y kyrcher rac carchar braw

Inquisitors create heretics

Wybren y bore'n aberoedd o waed
Yn hollt y mynyddoedd

Don't you see the oaktree flailing
Like a pulse against a pattern
Of disintegrating clouds
And dawns in the cleft of mountains
Making estuaries of blood?
No age or place for portents this
Or elegies that beg for thunder.
In the closed books all the poems
Wind along to neat conclusions.
Blackness presses on the river.
Air hangs still among the branches.
Drizzle licks to dullness pavements.
Fear's prison leaves no refuge.
At night that stillness always
And the flick of headlights on a
Hill signals distant travellers.
At night that stillness always
And wife and man not sleeping
Listen to the third one growing.
A hand on the distending womb
At night equivocates between
Blowing yeast in the kneader's palm
And a pulse like a ticking bomb.

*

As if in some jaded film
The smart men waited in a car
Watched the lights and checked the callers
Waited till the house was empty.
Only one and him they wanted.
Waited till the street was empty.
Only one and him they wanted.
Listen for the hand that knocks.
The rights read and the man taken.
Headlights pushed out through the darkness.

*

The fishman's head locks the cervix.
At night the voice sighs:
                    Most men lead
Lives of quiet desperation.
Onlooker and participant
I watch my life unwinding slowly
Fall along an ancient pattern.
Are you content?
                    I suppose so —
A world of supposing and slow
Acquiring.
              Are you settled?
Earthenware and furniture
Gather on us like dust. The work
Sucks like tapeworm, leaves enough
For sickly living.
                    Contentment
Shouldn't sound like that.
                              Contentment

Is to know that pain will go, or
Not. Anyway it doesn't matter.
In other words it's passionless.
I know that I am always moving
Where the worm wraps to the pattern
I know that I am always quite still
Watching where the worm is coiling
Like dark that's pressed upon a stream.
Onlooker and participant
I watch my life unwinding slowly.

*

Cellbeds stinking of drunks' vomit.
The caged bulb and the smeared teamug.
Images from some jaded film.
Threat. Warm chat. Humiliation.
Smart men take turns, ties loosened,
Soften up and prise at details.
Give him an hour on his own.
Remember never switch the light off.
The methods are all well established.
Nothing. Nothing. Nothing. Nothing.
You know where we can take you to?
Just kick the chair from under him —
Fear's enough to crack the bastard.
You must be careful what you think.
Listen to your own blood pumping.
Careful that you make no thoughtcrime.
Fear's prison leaves no refuge.

*

Seasons break the fusing knuckles.
I had thought that all the world
Would turn to bone like oak's heartwood
Sapless at the dark centre,
Maturity that stoniness,
We antlered like those standing trees
With fossil hearts in the still air.
Seasons rebreak fusing knuckles
In the turn from spring to autumn.
Eyeslits burst on growing copses,
Bindweed blossoming on cypress.
Eyeslits burst on bleeding autumn,
Slabs of light that sculpt the mountain,
Loose chevrons of the birds migrating
Pointing to a further purpose
Ravelled out across the sky.
The bunched heart unclenching
Feels the air stir in the branches
In the turning towards winter.
Onlooker and participant
Feels time prising at the eyelid.

*

The voice that drilled me in darkness
With questions of small desperations
Steady as the bombclock ticking
Has hushed me with this news. An old friend
Held and his life leaking away
Through the meshed catwalks, through gaps
Between the words on chargesheets, through
Thoughts that he should not have uttered.

Out of the quiet now the voice
Hisses afresh
>   *Conspiracy.*
Its sibilance coils in the skull
Wraps to the pattern of the thoughts
We'll soon be too afraid to say.

*

Pregnant women like piles of pears.
They suffer quietly in the
Last days in the spring warmth, lying
Behind their bellies, a book
Propped up, or wrestling their loads
Off the bedside to the door
Knuckles uncertainly brushing
One wall of the corridor.
These are strange countries. The map
Of veins slowly rent, reshaped by
New weight, the surface of each blown
Land exploding blotches, freckling
Ridges. The linea negra
Named like some buckling continent
Deepens arching from crater to
Gulch across the rising planet.
Earthmothers built like a darts team
Recline in purgatory, and,
Around the ward, shift elbows as
They feel flesh kicking in the egg.
   The vee of hair around the vulva
Pulses where the head's presented
Bulges like a lidded eyeball

Pulses to the mother surfing
Pain harnessed to the dancing needle.
Not quite yoked to moon and menses
Onlooker and participant
I find a place and egg them on.
And when the eyeslit bursts open
When lips part on the blind eyeball
When the hurt skull mushroom white
Stares blind in the tanned flesh slit
And rends the safe corridor,
Hands guide the swimmer's slipway
From one chamber to another.
The cleft and emptied figure gasps.
Blood and offal flood a delta,
A dawn in the cleft of mountains
Pointing to some firmer purpose.
The choked puce face unclenches
With the shock of air. Vein-boughs
Like rivers of light stretch fingers,
Pull back lids from new-white eyeballs.
Slabbed on the mother's belly he
Almost unsays inquisitors.
All things are cause for waking
To ourselves. Shaped by the seasons,
Politics, our children, see
Not bare trees wailing for dead kings
But the branching of arteries,
The softboned skull like a furled bud
Celebrating what we are.

*

Too much? A few bent coppers?
After all, he was acquitted —
Why shout so loud? We say that it's
Worse than this in other countries.
Because two years can't be brought back,
Because I felt the fear also
Closing on me like a prison.
Friend, it would be parochial
To pretend the action's elsewhere.
We have seen the live tree flailing
And the burning wedge of daylight
Pointing to a firmer purpose.
Listen for the knock of callers
To make you grow afraid to speak.
Listen for the hand that knocks
To make you grow afraid to think.
Listen for the voice that questions
Making winter in the mind.

This fragment was started when a friend of mine was held on a
charge of conspiring to cause an explosion. He was eventually
acquitted but by that time had spent over a year in prison.
Nyt oes le y kyrcher rac carchar braw — "There is nowhere to go
from the prison of fear" from 'Marwnad Llywelyn ap Gruffudd' by
Gruffudd ab yr Ynad Coch (thirteenth century).
Inquisitors create heretics — Umberto Eco.
Wybren y bore'n aberoedd o waed/ Yn hollt y mynyddoedd — "The
morning sky estuaries of blood in the split of mountains" from
'Cilmeri' by Gerallt Lloyd Owen.

1985

I met a friend.
I've been on strike, he said.
One year and then we lost. Cops
held me for a bit then let me go.
But I was innocent see.

I met a friend.
I've been away, he said.
They said I had a bomb. Remand.
One year. Then they let me go.
But I was innocent see.

And my friends said,
I know it was not what I did
it was not for the things I did
that they took me.
What I think and what I represent
are what they hate —

the blame's in what I am, not what I do.

And friend, since you call me friend,
where were you?

CHRISTENING POT BOILER

Chamber maid
or cabin boy
passenger
room taker
true squatter
womb liner
woman filler
menses stopper
vomit causer
quasi modo
crouched at bellmouth
belly burden
bone garden
meat tumulus
homunculus
extra pulse
fish fellow
flesh hoop
human coil
vein labyrinth
amnionaut
tethered selky
potence prover
cash remover
accident-
al occupant
multiplication
and addition
love's dower
placenta flower
blanket denter

bladder squasher
snug dweller
dug sweller
milk maker
udder flooder
tum tickler
mother kicker
sleep spoiler
pot boiler
caul crammer
wind jammer
blood swimmer
gore surfer
dam buster
home breaker
mess maker
distraught squaller
future crawler,
welcome.

MONSTERS

Cardboard-headed
I lumber on the lawn
searching all its angles for my son
and *beepo*. It's his turn.

He puts the box on.
A two foot zombie chases me
but soon gets tired, prefers
to be pursued, cackles while he runs, though
there's no escape on this cramped patch of green.

My turn again.
Inside, soft light penetrates
the cardboard's subtle buff
and intimate as the smell of binding
on a close-held book comes
the whiff of apples that once packed the box
far off
glimpsed like something gleaming in deep water.

The monster stops, tasting.

We take turns to play him, to know
the cramps and music of our island.

MARGAM PARK

Spring's first hot sun
electrum pale like some new minted thing
and we bring you smiling in the pram,
your older brother wanting space to run,
machine turned consumers.

Landscapers thought of rhythms, harmonies,
but the music's lost on us — it's
a space to play in for workers' kids,
shy deer fading into trees,
a lake and sculptures — steel or wood or stone —
scattered in the new-rich garden.
They aped the bandit lords in latticed
perpendicular, five centred arch of
ruined mock tudor. And beyond,
polished on the steely air
shimmering through petrol haze there gleams
the mirage of blast furnaces' retorts
immense along the bay.
They've still warm hearths — this folly's gone a shell.
Steel obelisks mock mock history,
say: we still spew for the owners,
though they've gone.

The coast's a motorway, a sewer web,
scurf of buildings that heave up and break,
us-infested. There's the truer monument
among the latticework of pipes,
spawning in interstices of roads.
We need none, walk into the light,
though for moments only, look up,
prehend the fabric of an outstretched sky.

I park your pram by a blank stone face,
your head, unmoving, moving me to know
it's people animate this space
sculpt time with passing here
no art but being human.
Soon, nothing but the kodacolor blur
of smiling parents, a selfconscious boy
and yourself asleep, that incandescence,
all that immensity of light suppressed
into a half or untrue smudge.

Your fringed shawl plays arpeggios on air.
A small hand flutters echoing the notes,
plays half a scale, tightens on the cloth.

OPENING TIME

I felt my flesh assembling on the bars, plates and scoops of bone. The muscles bunched into balls at the bases of my thumbs. Flaps of skin furled themselves on my shins. The jelly of my eyes came into being and fashioned itself into bulbs. There was a small twitching sensation in my skull as the nerves knitted themselves between reshaping brain and retina.

I have only a short recollection of this as the brain and other soft stuff, having rotted first, came back last.

There was no sudden quiver of life or anything dramatic like that. I was aware of my weight flattening my buttocks, my feet hanging to one side, twisting the relinked columns of bone, muscle, sinew and ligament in my legs. My jaw pulled up against its own weight, set the rows of teeth into their old bite.

My teeth.

The new tongue moved easily along the rows feeling them carefully and in my mind I made a picture of them. Real teeth, the gums overlapping them firm and unreceded.

The earth around my face was not pressing hard, had merely leaked through rotted patches in the lid perhaps. Or no, I thought, there must have been endless ages and all that would be gone. Still, it felt very loose.

I rolled my head slightly to one side, tried gingerly to raise a hand. There was no strain, no stiffness. I felt that the soil was gently gathering itself away from me. It parted to left and right from the centre of my chest. My face, I thought, was clear. Opening my eyes I glimpsed some fragments of mud pulling away from my eyelids. I got to my feet without feeling any effort.

All around me people were getting up out of the earth. In some places dozens rose out of a single space one behind the other, sometimes in pairs. The ground was pocked with shallow craters of loose earth endlessly disturbed by rising people. Some lay staring at the sky, which was not blinding bright but veiled with thin pale grey cloud; others jumped up and ran; some, like me, got up carefully and looked around. They mostly looked around twenty-five, though some looked younger. There were quite a lot of babies, some of them very tiny and bald. They, quicker than anyone, stood and ran, looking very happy, even the ones that scarcely looked old enough to have been born.

I looked at my hands and felt my face and hair. There were no wallets of withered skin on my wrists and neck. I had lips that curved out and were fleshy. The hair was thick over my skull. There were no liverish splotches on the backs of my hands. My knuckles were not swollen. My fingers flexed without clicking.

My wedding ring was gone. I looked down into the crater, from which more people were coming. My wife had not emerged with me. I recognized none of the people around me. We were all dressed the same, in clean, comfortably fitted suits made, somehow, of one piece of material which seemed to have no fastenings. The cloth was a pale pastel colour which I could not put a name to.

Still looking at my fingers, I began to walk with the others. Running, walking or stumbling, we all went in the same direction and although people sprang out of the earth everywhere the crowd was spread so that you could walk without being pressed faster than you wanted to go.

After walking a long time I came to two tall brick pillars which gave the impression of a gate. As I passed between them among others I looked back and saw, into the endless distance, the broken ground with young people and children still rising. When I was outside — it seemed as if beyond the pillars was outside — I saw that I was on a large plain of cinders. At a little distance it was neutral and colourless but underfoot it hinted at a dull, long-cooled red beneath the surface.

76

All around, as far as I could see, people ran or walked, still in the one direction. It might have been a trick of the perspective, but when I looked in that direction the crowd seemed to converge and the air above the centre of that horizon was tinged with a smirched orange pall.

I walked too, and tried to keep pace with a tall young woman with dark hair.

'Excuse me' I said. She did not look round, though I thought she had heard me. 'Excuse me, is this the right — '

I realized that I did not know what I wanted to ask.

She glanced at me and said something in a language I could not identify. I stopped and she went on, not looking back.

I watched the people streaming past me. What were the chances of finding one among them who spoke my language?

I noticed that a few people, like me, were standing still like fenceposts in a flooded river. Then I saw one young man walking in a different direction. Apart from that he was unremarkable, dressed as were the rest of us. I looked more carefully and saw another, a woman, I thought, walking against the flow. I walked sideways, so to speak, for a couple of dozen yards. It was not difficult. The walkers were well spread. From my new position I saw a few others walking away. I noticed that the children never walked anywhere but in the orthodox direction, and mostly more quickly than the others.

I turned and walked back through the crowd. If I had continued, I thought, the people would begin to bunch and I would be wedged, unable to turn.

Facing this way, I had the sensation that I was walking downhill, though I could see that I was still on the cinder plain. It was curious to look into the oncoming faces, some preoccupied, others smiling and without cares. For the most part they took no notice of me. One man paused and spoke words I did not understand, nodding to the place at my back, and then went on. I continued. Walking away was very easy and the feeling of travelling downward, despite the evidence of my eyes, persisted.

After a long time the crowd thinned further. The milky grey veil across the sky grew brighter. Somehow, so gradually that I did not notice it happening, my picture of walking on a plain and my sensation of descending adjusted to one another and I was walking down an undulating slope of cinders and shale. There were very few walkers passing me at this point and when the slope suddenly dropped very steeply before me, I realized there were none.

I half slid down the crumbling reddish shale and onto tussocky mountainside which continued downhill before me. Overhead the thin cloud was shredding like ripe white cloth, revealing the blue.

I knew the place well. I walked down the mountain over rushes and coarse grass onto a rough track, down to the familiar council estate on a lip of hill a few hundred feet above the valley bed. It was a sunny day in spring and it had rained recently so the air was scrubbed and all the colours were sharp. Even the drab brick of the council houses and their metal windowframes were precise and pleasing in the sharp light. Across the valley the other hill, ribbed with terraces lower down and patched with fir plantations and-moorland above, was darkened sometimes by the dragged shadow of a cloud. I plucked a grass and walked down to the estate.

In the top street were the usual dogs, the bus parked at the end of its route for a few minutes. I walked through a gap between the gardens to the next street, down past the rusting garages of corrugated metal and around the corner. I stopped at the fourth, familiar gate.

Under my shoes of nameless pastel, pale brown earth clung

between the tarmac chippings. The paint on the corner of the tubular steel gate was flaked in the remembered way making neutral reddish islands. I lifted the chain and went in.

The back door was open. On the back steps a white and tan cat, halfgrown, was sunning himself, licking a wrist with his claws flicked out. A film of milk was drying in a saucer nearby, which sat on a place where the ashes from the fire were tipped. At the end of the back garden a woman stood talking to a neighbour across the fence, which was of wire strung on concrete posts. She was youngish, wearing a headsquare and a pinafore, slippers trimmed with nylon fur. She rested one hand on the fencepost as she talked, and one foot rested on its toe.

I went into the house. In the frying-pan on the cooker were sizzling discs of black pudding. The gas was low so they would do slowly.

I recognized the pattern printed on the kitchen oilcloth. The place had the familiarity of a dream, though I knew I was not dreaming.

I walked into where I knew the livingroom would be. There was a newish fire in the grate, the lumps of coal vaulting a burning orange space. On the mantelpiece was a buff, square-faced clock, the salt and pepper pots. A boy aged about ten lay in front of the fire reading a comic, absorbed.

There came the smell of carbolic soap, the sound of breathing, slightly laboured. A man, youngish, had come into the kitchen and, glancing into the frying-pan as he passed, unbuckled the belt of his raincoat. He came into the livingroom, not looking at me, and put a food tin which he carried under one arm onto a table. The boy and he exchanged greetings. The man, as I knew he would, put a hand into his pocket and brought out a tube of sugared sweets. The boy took them saying thanks and went on reading, peeling back the silvered paper of the tube. The man stood watching for a moment as the boy put the first sweet in his mouth and champed at it.

I looked out of the window. People passed and on the far mountain a bus moved. All these people, I thought, except one, were walking towards an orange smirch in a milk grey sky, and I would have to go back up the hill and over the shale and across the cinders with them. I thought of the gritty chippings of sugar lodging between the boy's teeth and I knew that whatever was at the end of my walk, it could not be paradise.